Kangaroos

Steve Parish

KIDS

What has big ears...

...is covered in thick fur...

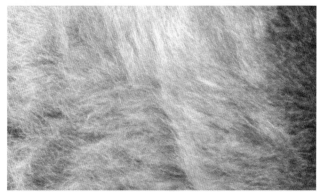

...and hops on its two back legs?

A kangaroo!

red kangaroo

Are there different types of kangaroo?

Yes! There are three types of kangaroo.

There are red kangaroos, eastern grey kangaroos, and western grey kangaroos.

eastern grey kangaroo

western grey kangaroo

5

Which type of kangaroo is the biggest?

Male red kangaroos are the biggest. A large male can stand as tall as a man!

How big are eastern grey kangaroos?

A male eastern grey kangaroo can grow almost as large as a male red kangaroo. He also has strong, muscular arms with long, sharp claws. Females are smaller.

Do all red kangaroos have red fur?

No. Female red kangaroos can have grey fur. Big males have rusty red fur, while young males can have light red fur.

How can I tell a western grey from an eastern grey kangaroo?

A western grey kangaroo's fur is brown with a few grey speckles through it.

What do kangaroos eat?

Kangaroos love to eat sweet, juicy grass, but sometimes they nibble the leaves of small bushes, or even bark from trees!

When do kangaroos eat?

Kangaroos like to eat when it is cool.

They eat early in the morning and late in the afternoon.

When do kangaroos sleep?

Kangaroos rest and sleep during the middle of the day when it is hot. They lie on the cool grass or under shady trees.

Do kangaroos live in groups?

Kangaroos live together in family groups called "mobs". A big mob can have hundreds of kangaroos living in it.

How does a kangaroo move quickly?

A kangaroo uses its strong back legs like giant springs to bounce along and quickly hop from place to place. A kangaroo hops quickly to travel long distances or escape from predators.

How does a kangaroo move slowly?

A kangaroo moves slowly when it is eating or when it doesn't need to travel far from place to place. It uses its front paws and strong tail for balance as it lifts its back feet up and brings them forward.

What is a baby kangaroo called?

A baby kangaroo is called a "joey".

Any baby animal that grows inside its mother's pouch is called a joey.

What does a joey eat?

When it is very young, a joey has no fur. It stays tucked away in its mother's warm pouch and drinks only her milk. Once the joey is bigger and has fur, it begins to poke its head out of the pouch and nibble grass.

How long does a joey stay in its mum's pouch?

A joey spends almost one year developing and growing inside its mother's pouch while it drinks her milk.

What is this joey doing?

This joey is too big to fit in the pouch, but it can still poke its head in for a drink of milk. At the same time there could be another tiny, hairless joey tucked away in the pouch, drinking milk and growing!

Why doesn't a joey bounce out of the pouch when its mother hops?

The pouch has a muscle at the top that tightens and pulls the top of the pouch closed. This holds the joey safely inside.

Does this joey still drink milk?

No, this joey only eats grass, but it stays close to its mother because it still has a lot to learn about growing up.

Why are these two kangaroos fighting?

Young male kangaroos living in the mob often playfight with one another. This is good practise because when they become strong, adult males they will need to fight one another to find out who will be the boss of the mob.

Do kangaroos have any enemies?

Kangaroos are big animals that do not have many predators, but sometimes they are hunted by hungry dingoes!

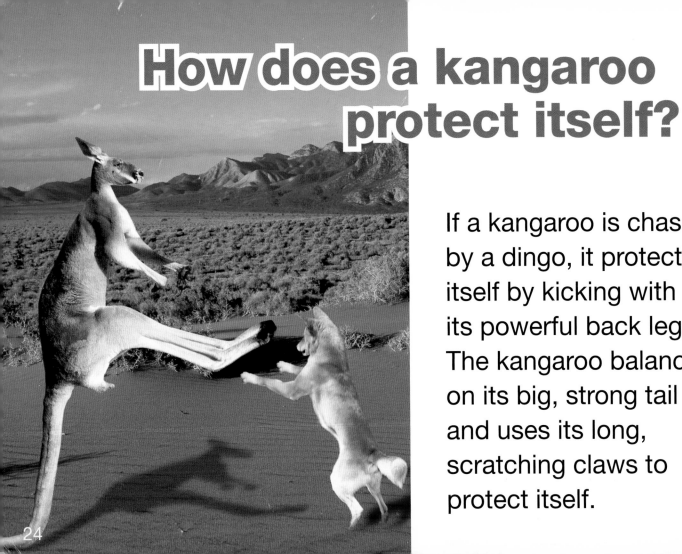

How does a kangaroo protect itself?

If a kangaroo is chased by a dingo, it protects itself by kicking with its powerful back legs. The kangaroo balances on its big, strong tail and uses its long, scratching claws to protect itself.